# Go for the Gold

# Go for the Gold

## Somebody has to lose...but why you?

by
Garry Hoyt

Illustrated
by the Author

Chicago
Quadrangle Books
One-Design & Offshore
Yachtsman Magazine
1971

*To the electric excitement when pored-over plans
and dull days of practice somehow come together
in a racing move that shakes you free of the pack;
. . . you cross the fleet and taste the sudden
silence and splendid loneliness of first place.*

# Contents

# Go for the Gold

# Five-Minute Warning

*L*et's face it, the world is not really waiting
for another book on sailing. And, alas, though I
have waited patiently, there has been no detectable
clamor from the throngs, no pressing public
demand that I share the priceless private percep-
tions that have led to my many dazzling wins.

In response to this thunderclap of silence, I
decided my only course was to bring forth a book
—conceived in audacity and dedicated to the
proposition that all men are created beatable.

This book will specifically not attempt what
would be a pointless duplication of information
already clearly established by such blue chip
sources as Elvström, Marchaj, Wells, etc. Rather, I
assume you have already read these fine authors.
If not, you should certainly begin by doing so,

because it is both foolish and costly to ignore the store of expertise they represent.

*Go for the Gold* is an attempt to jostle you into the realization that winning or placing better is, as much as anything, a state of mind, an attitude. This winning attitude is neither as simple as the power of positive thinking nor as complex as you have probably come to fear. My modest aim is to try to help you pull your game together, to home-in on those areas where just a small improvement will yield big yards, and places at the finish.

The title hints and urges at Olympic glory, and that is deliberate because I feel the Olympics are, in yachting, as in all sports, the very quintessence of quest.

I offer, not the dogma of a long-time winner, but the trials and errors of a committed challenger. It is my hope that this view from somewhere short of Mount Olympus may be closer to your lot, and that the style, unweighted by the certainties of solid gold accomplishments, may please where it cannot preach.

# Don't Kid Yourself

*M*ost sailboat races are not so much won by the winners' skills as lost by the losers' mistakes. It follows that improving your sailing performance is more a question of subtracting stupidities than of adding genius.

The first step in reducing stupidities is to recognize and label them as such. This requires cold realism and merciless self-appraisal. If there is one malaise that afflicts racing sailors in general, and losing racing sailors in particular, it is the inability to look failure in the eye and to link it correctly with blame.

Most of us go to elaborate lengths to blame our failure on the boat's performance rather than our own performance. This kind of evasiveness is entirely natural, and there is admittedly a satisfying amount of therapeutic solace to be had by roundly cursing the inadequacies of one's sails, rig, design, and hull. Next in the line of fire is the crew, whose well-recorded blunders are a rich lode of source material for diverting criticism. Perhaps most common of all is the fixing of blame on the perverse vagaries of an unkind fate, which has somehow singled us out for cruel and unusual punishment.

I recall a classic example of this "hand of God" syndrome in a snatch of conversation overheard at the Royal Bermuda Yacht Club.

A skipper, whose blackened mien proclaimed his non-success for the day, entered the bar after the race, muttering darkly and seeking alcoholic grace. "How'd you do today, Jerry?" asked someone brightly from the bar (there's always a smart ass at the bar who will ask this question). To which Jerry replied, with all the religious fervor of a truly wronged man, "I was shit upon . . . and from a great height."

Rationalizing a truth too painful to accept immediately is permissible for a while, and a commendable flair for creativity is frequently displayed in these postmortems at the club. But you must be willing, in the cold light of dawn, to put aside that folly in order to face and examine the real reasons, which are usually directly traceable to the SS factor—skipper stupidity.

Failure to face up to the SS factor is the biggest single block in the improvement of most sailors. By being unwilling to identify the real causes, they waste an inordinate amount of time looking for a more flattering or less damning place to dump the blame.

Local conditions are another favorite scapegoat for the nautical underachiever. A lot of guys bleed and bleat continuously about unreliable local conditions, the amateur ability of the local race committee, the outright favoritism toward the local boys, and so on and on. And I freely confess I have often joined this "we've been screwed" chorus. Because it feels so good, especially after you've finished so bad. Over the years I have observed that my tendency to complain varies in direct proportion to how high I place. When I finish well, it has generally been "a fair test" (even if it was a reach all the way). When I finish badly I've been victimized by an obvious conspiracy between maliciously inconsistent weather and manifestly incompetent local officials.

So okay. Shoot off, if you must, your big fat mouth, since that eases the strain which the facts might otherwise impose on your ego. But don't confuse this kind of lip therapy with a productive analysis of what really went wrong.

Any race, anywhere, is in some way a local regatta, with all the flaws and foibles pertaining thereto. You should study, understand, and compensate for these variations from the ideal, just as you study the local tides and weather. Because they are part of the test, whether they should be, or whether you like it, or not.

By this I do not mean that you need passively

accept poor or unfair race committee decisions. In the name of justice, progress, and everything noble, you must argue these causes. But a dispassionate review of the cases of sailor versus race committee will reveal an overwhelming preponderance of decisions favoring the latter. Whether this has to do with their actual correct behavior or their divine right as kings becomes fairly academic—them is the facts, which you can grieve about extensively but must live with in the end.

Since in this book we are concerned with getting you farther up on the scoreboard, I merely suggest we proceed realistically to that end, and ridding yourself of the yachtsmen's perennial persecution complex is an index move in that direction.

There is even a scientific principle which applies to all this—known as the "Law of Parsimony." This law, which surfaced sometime in the 14th century, says that you "cannot explain a behavioral phenomenon by a higher, more complex process if a lower or simpler one will do." Translated to sailing terms this means that your latest involved exposition on how a series of unforseeable and arbitrary factors combined to deny you first place must give way to the simple explanation that you "just blew it through good old S.S."

In summary, kidding others can be forgiven as just another human frailty, but kidding yourself is a fatal distraction from the basic task of getting to go faster.

# Boat Speed

*T*he quality known as boat speed is as elusive as the phrase itself is awkward. Like, what other kind of speed is there in sailboat racing? I suspect the prefix "boat" owes its origin and continuation to the defensive syndrome earlier discussed. We want to make it very quickly clear that our twenty-third place was directly due to the fact—obtusely beyond our control—that the damn boat just wouldn't go. So we quickly interject "boat" before "speed," lest someone begins to think along more personal lines, like "skipper" speed.

It seems more than coincidence that boat speed abbreviates to BS, and in most instances you can freely substitute the more common interpretation of those letters.

In any case, after skipper attitude, this speed we

shall call "boat" comes first, because you have to have it to win. By boat speed I mean the physical ability of your boat to move as fast as the rest of the fleet. Without boat speed, poorer sailors will beat you and better sailors will murder you. Without boat speed the shrewdest tactics fail, the most basic offensive and defensive moves founder, and race strategy reduces itself to a series of desperate gambles which are doomed by the odds to be largely unsuccessful.

On the other hand, get boat speed and you're in clover. Virtually everything you try will work better than it deserves to, and almost everything your opponents try will fail delightfully. So boat speed is worth striving for. Fortunately it is not the fickle abstraction that some would have it—here today and gone tomorrow.

"Today I just didn't have any boat speed" is a familiar refrain at Ye Olde Yacht Club bar. Remember the first commandment: that we not kid ourselves. Boat speed can be perversely dependent on delicate changes, but it is a state of attainable physical adjustment, not a mystical intangible.

You get boat speed by buying the best equipment, tuning it, and then keeping yourself reasonably unobtrusive at the controls.

What about tuning? There is a lot of unnecessary mystery surrounding and shrouding this subject. To begin with, the choice of word is perhaps unfortunate. "Tuning" brings to mind a musician listening carefully and then making minute adjustments on his piano or violin. The parallel

*Go for the Gold*

image in sailing is the nautical wizard bent over his craft making micrometer alterations to bring her into tune. That's a lot of crap, so forget it.

Let's admit that on this topic most of us have the uneasy feeling that accompanies incomplete knowledge. We observe with awe the greats like Elvström making, with the confidence of a surgeon, precise and apparently calculated scientific adjustments which somehow magically improve their speed. Then we stumble back to our own boats, numbed by our ignorance and psyched by the certainty that they're getting ahead of us again —and right there on land yet.

At this stage I usually polish the bottom of my boat, pursuing the faint hope that sympathetic stroking and mumbled incantations will somehow compensate for the awkward reality that I really haven't a clue to what else to do. Fortunately this mental blank is usually temporary, and not nearly so fatal as it might seem, because the percentage estimate of how much speed can be improved by minor tinkering is vastly exaggerated.

We need some basic definitions, so let's begin by stripping away the hokum about tuning terms. We're not talking about the hull. Buy the best hull you can afford, put it in shape, keep it right on minimum weight, sand it smooth before big races, and forget it. Nor are we talking about sails. Buy the best (even if you can't afford them), fold them carefully, and forget about them, too. You can't change them—that's the sailmaker's job. Trying to save money on sails is extremely false economy.

They're the engine, boy, so let's get all the horsepower we can.

By elimination we find that tuning really means the adjusting of mast position, mast rake, stay tension, sheet location, positioning of hiking straps, compass, bailers, barber hauls—in short, the certain kind of fiddling around with the gear that manages to make the boat and sails trim better or easier. I say "certain" because it must be obvious that if the right kind of fiddling around can make you go faster, the wrong kind can make you go slower. So don't fiddle for fiddling's sake, because you have at least a 50 per cent chance of doing the wrong thing.

Fortunately there are some ground rules for successful tuning:

1. Start with the best proven equipment. It's hard enough to get even the best equipment to work right. Trying to adjust uncertain equipment means adding another variable, which in this imprecise field you can probably ill afford.

2. Set your rig up the way the leaders in the class do. This sounds like pretty lame advice, but I guarantee it's the quickest way to get into contention with the leaders. The time for tuning innovation and experimentation is *after* you have reached par, not before.

*Trying to find tuning variations that will make them faster than the leaders is what keeps a lot of people slower than the leaders.*

It is true that you will never be a consistent

winner until you have developed the confidence to experiment freely by yourself. But don't expect this to happen right away. I repeat, the best way to reach par is not to pretend to a tuning knowledge that you cannot possibly attain in a short period. You don't need it, so why try to fake it? Start out by just copying the leaders in tuning and by concentrating on your sailing. This way you can postpone the complexities of tuning and you won't have those gnawing doubts about your boat's performance—which in turn tend to provide an all-too-handy haven for blame that should probably be laid to your sailing performance anyway. Set up your rig standard, and sail the hell out of it, without looking for the crutch of more speed than the others.

To understand why this is smart, you have to step back and get some perspective on the relative value of minor physical adjustments to your boat and rig. It is ten times more important to tune yourself properly than to fret about the last 10 per cent in that optimum 100 per cent efficiency in rig. You are by far the biggest variable out there, and the range of adjustment available to you via proper boat handling can compensate for any number of minor deficiencies in rig.

If there is a mystery about tuning, it is the magical bond that exists between a good skipper and the good boat he has come to know thoroughly. He senses her every mood and matches it to wind and wave. He hikes out at just the right instant before she heels, and comes in precisely when she eases. He coaxes her onto extra waves, and grooves his go-abouts to brief ballets. He gives the boat her head and never pulls her up short with jerky helm movements. He gains an easy rapport with fore and aft trim, shifting his weight in delicate rhythm like a surfer. His every move is marked by easy grace and knowledgeable anticipation. He's not just in the boat, he's with the boat.

Meanwhile his opponents scratch their heads, convinced that he has hit upon some breakthrough adjustment in rig. They will pursue this delusion, seeking the nonexistent touchstone, while the smart skipper concentrates on honing his own performance.

This may sound like an overly casual dismissal of the very real advantages to be had via correct adjustment of hull, rig, and sail. Of course you have got to have your rig right or you won't win. But put first things first. Given the best equipment, placed in the generally accepted positions, the properly tuned skipper will have little difficulty achieving par in boat speed. Better boat speed is a pot of gold most skippers pursue to the neglect of their more basic sailing skills, which have far more to do with a better score than any small technical adjustment in their rig could possibly yield. So set your boat up like the leaders, and try to beat them with their own adjustments. When you accomplish this, you will at least know that your sailing skill is an asset and not a penalty, and at that point you can begin to experiment

Go for the Gold

meaningfully with your own further adjustments and refinements in rig.

Tuning is not nuclear physics or advanced aerodynamics, and you don't have to be a mechanical engineer or a sailmaker to do it. What you're really aiming for is a developed sense of feel to measure changes against.

This sense of feel, plus the pragmatic comparing of equipment alterations against race results, is all you need to match the best. So forget the mumbo jumbo, and ignore the guys who are studiously pinging their stays. There are no two turns that will turn you into a winner, and there are no two turns that will keep you from being a winner.

Boat speed, like genius, is oft but perseverance in disguise. You must pay dues of frequent despair, but you can get it if you will grind away, mentally and physically.

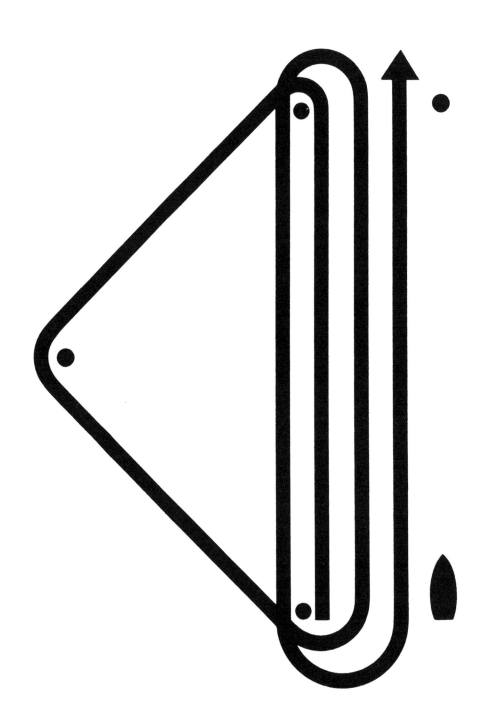

# The Olympic Course

*P*ractically every major regatta now uses the
Olympic course, because it insures a fair balance of
windward and leeward work. This new standardization in the patterns and personality of the course
invites a serious study of possible standard moves
and countermoves. Such a study was really not
feasible under the old setup, where a race course
could be almost any sequence of windward and
leeward legs as long as something of both was
included in the final mix.

The Olympic course is a kind of chessboard, and
there are some standard openings and ripostes
which you will pursue to your profit, and neglect to
your loss.

To recall the obvious, the Olympic course sets
up as follows:

1. Windward leg
2. Reaching leg
3. Reaching leg
4. Windward leg
5. Running leg
6. Windward leg

Though three of these legs are repeats, each one can be assigned different characteristics. The nature of each leg, and its sequence, has a direct bearing on its personality. For a simple example, the last windward leg is a distinctly different animal from the first. In the first leg you are surrounded by a large fleet probing an unknown field. Yet by the last leg you have around you a small, tired fleet pretty well tracking over routes of established advantage.

I believe that there is an identifiable structure and a distinct tempo to the average race over the Olympic course—that it tends to flow from tentative to aggressive to defensive, and that it pays to adjust your plans to these realities.

You will note from your own experience that far more positions change during legs 1, 2, 3, or 4 than during either legs 5 or 6.

So each leg does not share equal importance in *position change potential,* which is the subject that must concern you most closely.

For example, if you are leading or in the top three, your task actually becomes progressively simpler as the race evolves. There is increasingly less chance of interference, less chance of fouls, and you are free to choose the best course.

If you are an early leader, legs 2, 3, and 4 pose the most serious threats in terms of being overtaken. Correspondingly, if you are behind, your best chance to strike back is on legs 2, 3, and 4.

Your start and the decision as to which side of the course to play are the two big factors in the first windward leg. If you are good or lucky at both of these, you are bound to be in pretty good shape at the first mark (presuming equal speed). Then if you are a good reacher you will, on the next two legs, either widen out your lead enough to put the race virtually out of reach or close the gap enough to be hard on the heels of the leaders.

*Making nickels offwind is the real key to success on the Olympic course.* Somehow it doesn't get noticed as much as the windward work, but the opportunities for substantial gains are really much better offwind. Presuming equal dexterity in playing the wind shifts, it is very tough to close 50 yards to windward on pure speed, and you will be lucky to do as much in one whole leg. In contrast, just a few seconds of extra planing will net you 50 yards offwind. It is simply a matter of better return per time and energy invested.

I submit that the cautious starter and the mediocre reacher stand very little chance in a big fleet over the Olympic course. Conversely, the good starter and the good reacher will almost always be up there. It's a bit like having just a good serve and a good net game at tennis—not as good as a complete repertoire of strokes, but you'll win most of the games with it.

If you were to choose two areas where improvement would best show on the scoreboard over the Olympic course, you would direct yourself to better starting and better reaching.

I said earlier that the Olympic course is a chessboard. Maybe it's really a highly structured six-act drama, where the early impressions control the mood far more than most of us suspect.

# The Start

*T*he start of the race is much more than just the beginning of the action. It is your chance to get in the first punch, and as such it represents an enormous opportunity for loss or gain. If you blow the start, you must in consequence take the punch, or the punches. The passive acceptance of these early blows is what usually puts the average sailor initially behind, and harshly penalizes his whole first windward leg.

The average skipper lacks the confidence to jockey with the big boys at the line, so he settles for "being in there close at the start," and even deludes himself that this proximity approximates success. Nothing could be further from the truth.

The difference between a good start and a bad start cannot be measured by how many feet behind you are at the time of the gun. The real distance you lose by a bad start is a geometric progression of this. Because if you are behind in any kind of a fleet, you are, ipso facto, blanketed, or backwinded, or both. Thus you are doomed to spend the vital first minutes of the race going slower than the leaders, who are generally the ones you can least afford to give distance to. Moreover, your loss is multiplied, and your recovery hampered, by the fact that the most desirable courses are blocked to you by the occupancy of others.

Let's take a typical starting situation. The port end is slightly favored, so all the hot shots will be there. The lesser sailor stays away, figuring he'll be safer farther up the line. Sure enough, he starts farther up, maybe three seconds late, and in actual distance is only 25 feet behind the guy who hits the line at the buoy at the gun. Not bad, and he probably congratulates himself. But in sailboat starts, "not bad" usually means "not good," and so it is in this case. As a direct consequence of being three seconds late, our hero has to eat about two minutes of backwind, which costs him another 25 feet. Then he has to make several clearance tacks, which usually are out of sync with the shifts, so he drops another 25 feet. The result is that when the fleet first crosses after about four minutes, the leaders, by doing nothing more than sailing free and fast, already have a 75-foot lead delivered to them.

Now this 75-foot lead is not overly significant in itself, but it is pivotal in overall importance, because at this point Joe Average has two alternatives. The first is to tack behind and follow the leaders, and the second is to split and look for a different wind.

It is generally axiomatic that you don't catch the leaders by following them, but like all dogma this is dangerous when dogmatically applied. If the leaders are crossing on a lift (and they generally are), by splitting away you are only adding to their lead, pursuing the usually naive hope that the wind will be better on the other side. True, you might luck out over there, but seven out of ten times you won't, and then you'll find the leaders with 100 yards on you at the windward mark. Common sense should tell you that if the leaders are crossing on a lift, you better just calmly tack under them, concentrate on speed, and wait for brighter times.

But at this point the "not bad" start again reaches out to inflict one of its multiple penalties on the average sailor. Having seen the leaders spring—magically, in his mind—to a 75-foot lead, Joe Average is psychologically convinced that the leaders are just going faster and that correspondingly his only option is to split away and hope for a miracle. So he goes off on a loser and arrives at the windward mark seriously screwed. Then in the general jumble everybody fouls each other up around the mark and on the reach, while the leaders squirt farther out, free and clear, to a 200-yard lead. The rest is history.

In summary, the "not bad" start shackles your

performance on the vital first windward leg in the following intertwined ways:

1. Your speed is hampered by wind and wave interference.

2. Your range of good course choices is painfully narrowed.

3. You are distracted by clearance tactics as opposed to overall strategy.

4. You are denied the alongside stimulus of front-running competition.

5. You are psyched by the substantial early lead that the sum total of all these handicaps delivers, free of charge, to the leaders. And because of this, you are unduly tempted to take a flyer in order to recoup—and that generally puts you into the deep tank, from whence there is no return.

What about the converse benefits of the good or perfect start?

1. The range of good choices is as open to the front runners as it is closed to the backsliders. You get 100 per cent mobility to go where the best wind is.

2. You can go at full speed right from the start, unhampered and undistracted by wind or wave interference.

3. Best of all, virtually half the fleet will destroy themselves behind you.

Okay, we can certainly all agree it's great to have the best start, but the question then becomes —how? The features of a good start are, in order of importance and presuming a reasonably square line:

- Being on the line at the time of the gun
- Having clear air
- Being at the favored end of the line
- Having good speed at the gun

Of course, it's no good having just one or two of these features—you really have to put them all together for a great start. But if you have to give away something, do it from the bottom of that list rather than the top.

This advice may seem to contradict some fairly sacred precepts. Since the beginning of my sailing days, I was taught to be sure to be moving at the gun. Obviously that is the ideal. But if the price for being on the line at the gun, at the right spot, is to be dead in the water—I'll pay it in any of the modern dinghies. Because you can accelerate so quickly. Clearly this advice does not equally apply to keel boats.

Having clear air gets the nod over being at the favored end of the line, if that choice has to be made. In reality you never have to select one totally at the expense of the other. But on a good line, where the amount one end is favored over the other is slight, being able to move free and clear from the start is worth more than being exactly on the best end.

The extent to which this advice is true varies from class to class. In small, fast boats like the Sunfish and the Finn, you can clear your wind with

relative ease by bearing off and driving to leeward
—with the loss of only 15 or 20 yards. So it is
not quite as critical to be absolutely free and clear
at the start. But in keel boats, like the Tempest,
if you are backwinded and try to hold on, you will
lose 50 yards in very short order, and that isn't the
end, because by then you fall into someone else's
zone of influence—and the grief goes on. So clear
air in that kind of boat is particularly vital.

The favored end can mean either the end closest
to where the wind is coming from or the end which
best takes you to a favored spot. If you have reason
to expect a header off the land which is to the
port side of the course, then you want to go there
fast and first—so you pick the port end even if it is
not the favored end in terms of wind angle.

Okay, okay, that's great theory, but how do we
do it?

Perhaps the first thing you must do is develop
an aggressive or, perhaps better, an assertive
attitude at the start. Being assertive will not guarantee a good start, but being not assertive will
almost certainly guarantee a bad start.

Do not confuse calculated assertiveness with
reckless boldness, which is really entirely the
opposite. Aggressiveness in sailing, as in most
sports, is a question of balancing the risks and the
rewards. Top pro quarterbacks are fully capable of
making the big play from virtually anywhere on
the field, yet they are guided by the percentages
and generally go for the safe shots, only seeking
the out-and-out winner when the circumstances

are either so favorable, or so desperate, that the risks are justified.

In this regard I have read that if you are starting properly you will be over the line in one of three starts. I endorse the enthusiasm of this approach, and such a policy may be fine for small regattas at the club, where going back may cost you no more than 25 yards. But being over the line in, say, the Finn Gold Cup, with 190 hardy competitors thirsting for your blood, is a sobering prospect. If you are over, you will be lucky to lose less than 100 yards, if you get back at all. So aggressiveness at this risk is not really justifiable.

The most basic skill in good starting is learning to steel yourself to wait. It's a lot simpler to go tearing off on long reaches, but doing that merely stretches your ability to estimate correctly the distance to go versus time remaining, and it also leaves the field open for cooler hands to stake out their positions.

Unconsciously, in the minds of everyone, the boats that line up early become the pivot points around which other boats position themselves. The more you wait, the more pivot points you have to accommodate. By significant pivot boats I specifically do not mean those that arrive 'way too early at the line, accompanied by a great flapping of sails. These are generally skippered by erratic operators who eliminate themselves by their eagerness and go charging off down the line and out of contention.

The guy who early in the game lines up his

particular area of choice, protects it against the encroachments of intruders, and creeps slowly to the line usually gets the best start.

As a general rule, with one minute to go you should always be pointed at the line, with no more than 30 seconds of full-speed sailing distance to go to your desired spot. Now is when assertiveness comes into play. There will be those who will try to ride over you. Any time before 30 seconds to go you can let them pass. They will by their own momentum go over or off to leeward. But be careful of the guy who pulls slowly alongside to windward—he must be deftly luffed back to a respectful distance. The real threat is of course the guy who dips under your stern and comes up to leeward, or the guy who sails straight up from behind to leeward.

*The best guarantee of a good start is to make sure you have a cupcake to leeward.* This situation is so good it should be actively sought out. If you can flank yourself with two cupcakes you know you can beat, you are in the best of all possible worlds—you can proceed as if under convoy to the perfect start. This is a thing of beauty and light, available only to those righteous enough to deserve it, or devilish enough to preempt it.

When the best start is to be right at the port end, you are faced with a rather dicey choice. Only one guy gets this "best" start, and it's usually the guy who comes in at the last moment on port and tacks right to leeward of the approaching pack on starboard. This leeward and ahead position is great because you can luff up and then bear off full tilt for the barrel in the last five seconds. Here you can really go for it because your perception of where the line really is, is good at the port end, whereas elsewhere this is almost impossible to judge accurately.

Also, the penalty for being over early is not as heavy at the end of the line, because you can simply jibe around the buoy or committee boat and cross on port without losing much.

Big fleets mean bigger rewards for good starts and bigger penalties for lousy starts. Scratch and scramble, bluff and bluster, you have to get your place in the sun, because the alternative is just too tough.

The start sets the style and stacks the odds. Don't be shy and don't be tardy.

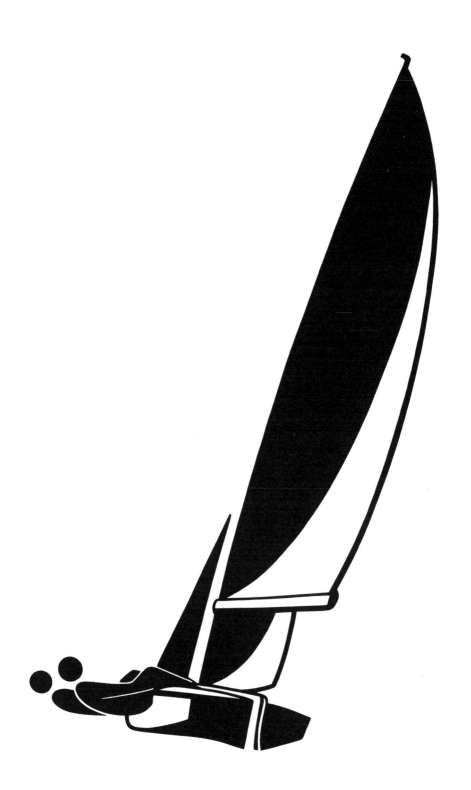

# Working to Windward

*A*bility *to windward* is traditionally revered as the true test of sailing skill. We visualize the grizzled salt beating into the blustery northeaster, amazing mere mortals as he drives his trusty sloop into the very eye of the wind.

This aura of nautical glamour surrounding windward work probably goes back to the days when the boats were at best uneven performers to weather, and being able to beat better was what kept you off the rocks or away from the pirates.

The truth is that today, in modern class boats, windward is probably the easiest leg to sail reasonably well. One of the first steps in doing it well is to treat it with a matter-of-fact respect, but absolutely no awe.

After all, the idea is fairly simple. You set your

sails to an angle of predetermined efficiency (the tried and true locations are common knowledge in all major classes), you fill away to get the boat moving, and then you see how high you can point without losing speed. The harder the wind blows, the higher you can point, and the softer the wind blows, the more you must ease off. Sound is your speedometer, and the tempo of the bow wave and luff of the jib tell you instantly whether you are accelerating, holding, or slowing down. Got it? Good, because that's all there is to basic windward work.

The three extra areas that usually determine a small boat's success or failure to windward have very little to do with the above fairly simple mechanics, which nearly everybody masters at a fairly early stage of sailing. If you haven't been scoring well to weather, it's probably not for lack of the Mosbacher touch, but for the more prosaic neglect of one or more of the following basic "extras."

### Hiking

Everybody in small boats lets the boat heel too much, and those who sin least in this direction are inevitably up near the top. You can have the finest bottom finish and the best rig, tuned to the nth degree, but if you let your boat heel, even just in the puffs, all these sophistications are for naught.

In 90 per cent of the cases, the boat that is sailed flattest is the boat that is sailed fastest. Since hiking is what keeps a boat flat, the ability to hike long and hard is the first, and the most frequently neglected, basic element in windward success.

## Pointing

Most people are really close-reaching half of their time to windward, and they are spared the embarrassment of this disclosure only because the bulk of the fleet is failing likewise. Any idiot can make the boat go by bearing off a bit—the trick comes in making it go while heading up a bit. We have made such a fetish of "not pinching" that we've forgotten the art of pointing. If you expect to win, you have to learn how to point higher while sailing just as fast—or, more accurately, to gain 10 per cent in windward distance while giving up only 5 per cent in speed.

## Threading the Waves

One of the remarkable things about the Acapulco Olympics was the way any number of top-flight Finn skippers just never got going. People like the former Olympic Gold Medal winner, and the then current Gold Cup winner, were never even in contention. The boats and sails were as nearly identical as they could be made, and yet these battle-tested skippers were 'way off form. The common complaint was the peculiar "chop on a swell" which seemed to baffle many. If you chose to concentrate on the chop, you missed the rise and fall of the swell, and I think this dilemma trapped many into fatal compromises which gave them the penalties of both without the solutions to either.

There is a pattern to all wave action, and the difference between fighting and fitting the pattern is enormously important. Alas, I have no scientific formula to give you. Maybe the best demonstration is to take a small rowboat and row with it into a windy chop at roughly the tacking angle. Then you will feel firsthand how the waves slap you around. Of course, when sailing you can quite easily counteract this with the rudder, but this sawing your way to windward is precisely what we want to avoid. The idea is to slip your way through, rather than bash your way over or hack your way around. This takes cunning, concentration, and a scrupulous desire not to get wet.

Maybe this is why the Scandinavians are so good to windward. They get an ice-water douche every time they blow a wave entry—and, man, that makes you careful.

### Adjusting the Rig

One of the great breakthroughs in recent years has been the discovery and development of various combinations by which you can induce and control mast bend, and adjust sheeting angles via travelers or barber hauls. I won't go into these here, because the subjects are specifically better covered in numerous articles by the various individual class experts, and general advice is definitely second best to specific advice when fooling with your rig.

# The Perils of the
# Inside Lift

*T*he great circle route **may be the shortest way** across the oceans of the world, but it sure doesn't work out that way on the race course. To be on the outside fringes of an inside lift, slowly rounding up to a seemingly endless orbit of the mark, while your competitors on the inside charge for it, is one of yachting's most exasperating disasters.

The only way this tragedy can be averted, or partially nullified, is by early discovery and immediate surgery.

When that first routine glance over your shoulder shows the windward competition heeling and pointing up to a new breeze, a little automatic alarm should go off, and you should brace for a dose of bitter remedial salts.

The temptation is to wait for the wind to shift

back, so you can cross on a lift, or at least not have to cross on a loser. If you're dealing with a normal oscillating shift, all well and good to wait. But if you are facing a genuine, full-fledged, communist-inspired inside lift, you'd best hustle your ass over there in a hurry. Because the longer you wait the worse it gets.

If you are among the favored few who find themselves partially on the inside of the lift, don't count your chickens too soon. Many's the time when, chuckling with glee, I have watched competitors come across on losers and pass comfortably behind me. Only to discover, minutes later, that by taking those losers deeper into the inside lift, they have neatly recouped and reversed the situation.

A basic maxim is not to take the tack which takes you behind your rivals, since that validates their lead. The inside lift is a definite exception to this rule. Whereas most tacks and changes of course are undertaken with at least the possibility of gain in mind, you tack back into a new wind with no illusions of profit—you're just trying to cut or control your losses.

One of the toughest things to learn, and something that the inside lift sharply demonstrates, is that it is far better to eat a little now than a lot later.

# Reaching

*T*he *reach* used to be the leg where all the boats were roughly the same speed—where you headed for the buoy, steadied down on course, let out the sails until they looked good, broke out the beer, and relaxed a bit. "A parade," it was called, and nobody really expected to gain or lose too much unless he had a real dog of a boat.

This anachronistic attitude persists to varying degrees in different classes. But the smart guys have long since realized that reaching is where you make it. Because in modern boats the difference between excellent and average means a far bigger payoff in yards on the reach than the same difference in ability could possibly yield to windward.

Figure it out. In a planing boat, the reaches are where your speed scale opens up dramatically. To windward the range of possible speeds goes from, say, one to five knots. With a steady blow, the difference between an average and an excellent performance might be 4.0 knots versus 4.3. Only a rare and gifted skipper is able to coax that extra .3 knot advantage over the fleet to windward.

But on the reaches your speed range is wide open. You can go from eight to 15 knots in a blink, and an excellent skipper can hold, for long bursts, a five- to 10-knot advantage over the average skipper. That's the kind of speed differential that can very quickly put you in or out of business.

The rub, of course, is that excellence in reaching is an elusive quality—as hard to analyze as it is to acquire. And you can have it and lose it, because it depends on stringing together a lot of related skills. The chapter on surfing becomes very pertinent here, because harnessing the waves is about 30 per cent of the story, and surfing considerations must be woven into every move on the reaches and on the runs.

Whereas to windward you think of maneuvering to minimize the effect of waves, on a reach you must maneuver to maximize wave effect. Remember the waves are with you now, and only a jerk of a skipper would overlook their willingness to help.

I am tempted to say that what you need to play the wind and the waves in successful harmony is a sense of feel. Except I seem to remember reading that in a lot of books, and being mildly frustrated. What's a sense of feel and how do you get it?

Well, you don't get it by reading. No way. A

movie would be a lot better than a book, because you could see the necessary interaction between sail trimming, weight moving, and wave playing that goes into building an extra edge in reaching. But let's at least grope for a description.

If you merely want par, you should plan on a minimum of activity, because any time you start moving around in a boat, your chances of fouling things up are at least as good as your chances of improvement. The average hacker makes just enough well-intentioned but inept moves to trip himself prematurely off a plane. Or to impose the steady drag which non-synchronized helm changes, non-precise sail trim, and incorrect weight-positioning combine to provide.

The next step up is the guy who lets his boat perform. He doesn't get in the way of the boat's basic willingness to sail well. He keeps the boat on her feet and in basic trim. The step above all this—the optimum—is the guy who lifts his boat to perform beyond what she could do for herself. By dipping off onto waves a little sooner and goosing the boat to stay on waves a little longer, by heading up almost imperceptibly when the wind softens and easing back down when it freshens, by jerking brutally on the mainsheet and helm when it is necessary to generate thrust, and by synchronized hiking, fore and aft as well as in and out—by doing all these things in symphony, the real reacher works his way inexorably through the fleet. To the confusion and chagrin of those who still believe that reaching is where you head for the mark, let out the sheet until she luffs, and then trim back slightly.

If you are out after excellence, forget about relaxing—reaching is a time for super-intense activity and concentration. Since you go faster on a reach, you have less time than on the other legs, and therefore you must pay even closer attention than you would to windward. On a reach your "position change potential" is concentrated. There are more yards to be gained or lost per minute— and fewer minutes available.

My conclusion is that fast reaching is first of all the best insurance policy you can have out on the course, but beyond that it is the most important single racing ability you can acquire, indispensable to any hopes of success in a serious sailing league. I wish I could be more explicit as to how to build reaching speed, but if I did nothing more than establish the primacy of reaching skill, this chapter would have proved something.

It's a bad pun, but a good point, that if you really want that gold you will have to reach for it.

# Reaching Tactics

*S*o *far* we have talked about reaching in terms of speed. Tactics also come into play, but this can be simplified to saying that tactical considerations on the reach should all be geared to leaving yourself free to sail faster. There is nothing more costly than being pinned below a slow reacher, or bearing off too soon so that a flock of early high riders choke off your wind supply.

It is insidious the way windward boats penalize you on a reach. Insidious because you never fully realize how much they are affecting you. The slow boats will hamper you, and the fast boats will hammer you if you let them above you. In most cases you can forget about breaking through to leeward unless the wind is strong and steady and unless you can drop off about 50 yards to leeward of the boat you want to pass—without going way below the next mark. If you have to drop off considerably below the next mark to get free air, forget it—because chances are you'll end up screwed.

As a general policy, if you've got the speed, it's better to claw up 50 yards to windward of the whole fleet and then try to blast over everybody—as opposed to running up to and around each boat. Boat-to-boat combat is usually too expensive on a reach—it keeps you from the sustained planes and long surfs which mean the big yardage.

If you are bidding to pass someone on the reach, don't try to pass close. This will infuriate them, and tease them with the possibility that a sharp luff might stop you.

Conversely, if someone comes up to you and tries to pass close aboard to windward, let him know very quickly that you are going head to wind rather than let him pass. It's just too costly to let somebody ride over you. He takes your wind and leaves you bobbing in his wake, and about that time somebody else picks you up and repeats the cycle.

For roughly the first two-thirds of the reaching leg, your course should be governed by the speed and direction which will net you the most distance gained. For the final third you must think in terms of how many boats you are actually going to gain. Buoy room then becomes a decisive factor. This is particularly true on the second reach, where a bad buoy-room position will leave you badly in the lurch and to the lee of the boats rounding up inside to the windward course.

The best reaching tactic of all is not to get involved in tactics. Remember, you're supposed to be going faster than anybody, and you have to be free and clear to do that. Maneuvers can only slow you down. The reach is the straightaway, and then's when you want to floor it and go.

# Surfing

*A lot of sailors* talk about surfing their boats, but very few really understand the subject. Of course any boat that is sailed before wind and wave will periodically be caught up by the waves and shoved ahead, willy nilly. This is accidental surfing, which can be very gratifying but should not be confused with the real art—getting on the waves sooner, and staying on them longer, than the rest of the fleet.

It is not a well-appreciated fact that, while you are surfing, you are sliding rather than sailing and you should be steering and moving in quite different ways than your normal reference to the wind would indicate. In classic surfing conditions you are using the wind only to get you on the wave and then to pick you up again when the wave drops you. The wind becomes auxiliary power rather than primary power.

By "classic surfing conditions" I do not necessarily mean a howling gale with huge, rolling swells. When the wind gets very strong, the possibilities of pure planing tend to intrude—you have to be guided as much, or more, by what the wind does as what the waves do. In these conditions it is generally best to aim for a constant plane, with just minor rather than major deviations for riding waves.

In all cases the faster you are sailing, the easier it is to surf, and when the wind offers planing possibilities, often the best thing you can do for surfing potential is to get up on a plane, stay on a plane, and just dip and weave over the crests as they come.

But let's go back to the basics. The best way to understand how you can get the most out of a wave is, not surprisingly, to do some surfing. Start with body surfing, which is both entertaining and instructive. This will teach you that catching a wave calls for a short maximum physical effort at the early stage, but that, once on the wave, guidance and technique are what keep you on or put you off. If you surf with fins, which is a damn sight easier, you will see that a timely spurt of kicking will keep you on the wave when it starts to lag, whereas otherwise you would merely be dropped. If you observe other surfers, you will see that some guys seem to be able to milk a wave right down to a ripple while others get dropped much earlier. Keep all this in mind because it eventually translates to sailboat surfing.

Body surfing, even if you are unsuccessful at it, will show you the feel of a wave better than anything I know. You will observe that, because your body is a relatively inefficient surfing shape, body surfing is pretty much a question of straight rides right with the wave—you are in the wave rather than in front of it or on it. By this system you go as fast as, but no faster than, the wave itself moves forward.

For the next step you really should try a surfboard. This sounds like a difficult and farfetched assignment, but it is not necessary that you be graceful or even proficient—only that you try it. Or failing that, you should observe other surfboard riders closely.

Simply stated, there are four primary steps for a good surfboard ride.

1. The wave picks up the rear of the board.

2. The surfer gives a powerful arm stroke and shifts his weight quickly forward (jumping to your feet has this effect).

3. The board drops down the face of the wave and the surfer turns away from the break in order to stay in the cleaner wall of the wave rather than the confused foam of the break.

4. The surfer maneuvers back and forth all over the wave by shifting his weight.

The third point is particularly important to a surfer. If you ride straight off you will plunge immediately to the bottom of the wave, where you run into the still water ahead and slow down sharply. The wave then breaks behind you and catches you again, shoving you forward inside or slightly ahead of a wall of foam. This is a relatively slow, mushy ride compared with the opportunities when you angle off on the clean wall. When you surf the wall, you are in effect sliding across a moving hill and theoretically you need never reach the bottom. As can be seen in the diagram, surfboard A travels a good deal faster than surfboard B because it travels a greater distance in the same time (the wave obviously gets from A to B at the same time all along its length).

SINCE WAVE ARRIVES HERE ALL AT ONCE

So by turning on the face of the wave you dramatically increase your speed, and also probably increase the length of time you are on the wave, since by going faster you have a much better chance to coast through the flat spots and squeeze the wave for all it's got.

The fourth point is instructive because it shows

what can be done with weight shifting. The surfer takes his standing position, not to look like Duke Kahanamoku, but because this is the position that best enables him to control trim.

All of which is elementary, and therefore generally unappreciated.

If you're still with me, let's see how all this applies to sailboats.

1. As the wave picks up the stern of the boat you need a shot of extra speed (the equivalent of an arm thrust or kick thrust). This is accomplished by rapidly trimming in on the sheets. Let's not say trim—that sounds like a 12-Meter. You haul, almost jerk, the sheet in.

2. At the same time that the stern lifts and you haul in sheets, you must shift your weight sharply forward. At this point the bow will often seem just about to bury in the wave. Pay no heed, and resist the temptation to move aft. The bow is down only because the stern is up, and if you shift your weight forward it will pop out even more quickly. Many people move aft, which slightly lifts the bow but also loses the wave. This final forward thrust can be achieved by either leaning forward, or by raising your tail and "ooching" forward—or by actually moving your whole body forward from one spot to another.

3. Once you feel the wave grab you, turn your boat to slide along the face of the wave rather than straight down the front of it. Remember that you should not limit this turning to an upwind

swing—you can bear off on a wave just as often as you head up. In fact, when you are on a wave you can sail by the lee with impunity, and this is often very helpful in saving yourself a jibe. If you want to jibe, about the safest time to do it in heavy winds is when you are on a wave. The sail comes across like a marshmallow because there is little or no wind pressure.

It is possible to get very scientific about the motion of water particles within a wave, and a certain amount of theory is useful. Remember that despite the visual impression of a sweeping forward motion, the actual water particles within a swell are pretty much staying in the same place. It's a little like laying out a long piece of rope and then flipping it up from one end; you'll send a ripple or wave all along the rope, but nothing really moves forward. A practical illustration that a wave is not a moving stream of water is the fact that you retain excellent steering control while on the clean face of the wave. If the boat were merely going forward with the water, steering would be very slow and mushy—as it is within a breaker or in a stream.

To sailors on inland or protected waters, all this talk about swells and breakers may seem pretty academic. And of course on many lakes surfing is only occasionally possible, and therefore of limited value.

But even when the waves are very small, and amount to chop more than swells, surfing is possible and can pay big dividends. The real point, though, is that you will sooner or later face an important series on open water, and if you can't surf you're dead, because others can.

Learn to ride the waves, because it's super fun and because there's gold in them thar hills.

# Each Class Is a Classroom

$\mathcal{N}$o *class* is an island, above and beyond the others, and every sailor in every class would be the better for testing his skill in new environs. Thus it is unfortunate to see people limiting themselves to just one class, particularly when they make this insularity insulting by adding a smug sense of class superiority.

The Star class skippers for a long time let it be known, officially and unofficially, that they were the world's best class with the world's best sailors. They were sustained in this modest claim largely by the questionable evidence of their own applause. But because they said it often, and with impeccable assurance, their claim began to take on a certain legitimacy. And since the self-awarded aristocracy provided a convenient reason for disdaining the outside competition, which was also the only thing that could disprove it, they built themselves quite an image. The 5.5's also picked up this bit, and somehow were able to translate "spending power" to read "sailing skill."

No one argued that there were many excellent sailors in these classes. What galled was the abrasive Aryan arrogance of it all. Plus their undemocratic unwillingness to mix it, man to man, out in the alley.

So it was with a great sense of vindication that the small-boat sailors of the world saw Paul Elvström smite the philistines from their pedestals by almost casually toppling world championships in the Star and the 5.5. And—oh, sweet revenge— he did it to them by frequently employing dinghy tactics like sailing by the lee, and other little peasant pursuits that the aristocrats had missed by not looking beyond their noses.

Elvström is the best single example of the synergistic benefits of competing in a variety of classes. He was better in each because he was better in all. He did not try to protect his prestige and reputation in a hothouse atmosphere, but risked them freely in all the toughest classes. And won. Now *there* is a sailor!

The benefits of switching classes are more than just technical. It happens to be great fun to learn the quirks and idiosyncrasies of different boats. You will also find that each class emphasizes some particular skill, and if you learn that class you will have learned that particular skill better than anyone who has not sailed that class.

For example, the Finn teaches you to hike like no other boat, and you get to relate mast bend to sail draft to hiking strain in a most memorable equation. The Snipe will teach you windward tactics as well as any, because it handles beautifully on the wind, and all the adjustments are there with easily observable results. The Sunfish will show you surfing and the need to keep windward peace with the waves. I am just now tackling the Tempest class, and find it most different and instructive. If you have never sailed a big Inland Lake Scow or a catamaran you don't know what acceleration is. And so on with other classes and their particular virtues.

What keeps a lot of sailors from trying new classes is the fear of losing face. Maybe you are the club champion in Blue Jays, and you are not particularly anxious to dim the luster of that achievement with a twenty-ninth place in the Flying Dutchman. This natural reluctance is not helped by the inevitable wise guys who infect every class, the kind who will say "Hey, there's that Blue Jay hotshot, and he could only make twenty-ninth." He and the other underachievers of the class will then, after a few beers, extrapolate your twenty-ninth place in the Flying Dutchman versus your first place in Blue Jays to a mythical relationship which proves that Dutchman competition is tougher and that they, the underachievers of Dutchman, are therefore as good as the winners of other classes.

*Each Class Is a Classroom*

This tortured reasoning proves nothing more than the shallow talents of those who indulge in it. Granted, there are some small and obscure classes where winning is certainly easier than in other larger and more popular classes. But before you snicker at any class, better make sure you can get out and beat them on the water. In all likelihood, even if you win you will acquire a new respect, and you will always learn something.

Put your pride on the line in a new class. Your ego may take a few whacks, but you will find yourself forced to innovate where in your own class you might rely on habit—and a far stronger sailor emerges.

# The Sunfish

There are some 75,000 Sunfish in the world, making this easily the largest one-design class going. Unfortunately, the Sunfish cannot claim to be truly world-wide in distribution, since the class is almost exclusively located in the Western hemisphere.

All Sunfish are made by the Alcort Company, a fact which could be described as a mixed blessing. On the positive side, a single production source makes the class truly one-design. And severely restricting any fiddling with the gear means that virtually all the emphasis is placed on how the boat is raced, rather than how it is prepared for racing. The boats are so nearly identical that one can reasonably expect equal performance from any Alcort Sunfish hull. As an example, the boat I used in winning the world championship in St. Thomas came right out of the box, and I had never sailed it before. This kind of standardization is a very desirable feature, because it enables visiting skippers to compete with borrowed boats at no disadvantage.

Sunfish sails also are produced by just one company, and any alterations must be made by that company. This makes it unlikely that anyone will come up with a super sail, and obviates expensive experimentation.

On the negative side, company control has often been less than imaginative. Pointless inflexibility has failed to take advantage of the many new improvements in building materials, and subsequent gains in the efficiency and weight/strength ratio of racing fittings. In short, company policy has lagged behind technical progress. The Sunfish is stocked with a number of Mickey Mouse fittings which are in general undersized, or overweight, or both. These fittings could be improved at no increase in cost, with a considerable increase in efficiency and ease of control.

However, none of these complaints alters the basic fact that the Sunfish is a most satisfying little boat, remarkably sensitive and classically simple. And while virtually no changes are allowed on the standard equipment, a lot can be done to make your Sunfish perform to its maximum potential.

### The Sail

It is possible to agonize endlessly over the many variations in the supposedly standard sails that come from Ratsey. The problem starts with the cloth, which looks to be about the cheapest dacron available and will not hold shape in the manner one has become accustomed to in the other classes. But no matter, everybody has the same problem, and while others are stewing about it, you might as well make the best of it.

The first thing to accept is the reality that these sails have very little shape cut into them. Just lay some new sails on the floor and you will very quickly see that they are flat. Only a little round has been cut into the luff and the foot. Yet somehow when you hoist them, they assume a shape of sorts.

Since these Sunfish sails are basically flat, your first concern in normal winds should be to not flatten them any further. Let's consider the various controllable elements which could possibly contribute to Sunfish sail shape.

1. Tension along the gaff
2. Tension along the boom
3. Location of halyard on gaff
4. Location of gooseneck ring on boom
5. Traveler adjustment

Taking these items in order, think about tension along the luff. It may be helpful to think of the gaff as merely a raked mast, and forget about the actual mast—which is fixed and really only serves as a support column to hold up the gaff.

Once you visualize the gaff as the mast, you can see that tightening the luff moves the belly

The Sunfish

forward, which is right for heavy winds, and that loosening it moves the belly aft, which seems to be better for lighter winds. There is certainly nothing revolutionary about this, but most of us forget how sensitive this adjustment is on such a small boat. I would caution that many people often leave the luff too loose in an attempt to get more draft in the sail. This merely creates a scallop effect along the gaff, which I believe loses more in vital leading-edge sail shape than it may gain in adding draft.

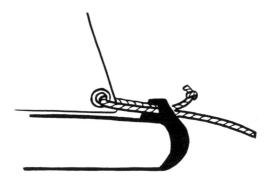

HOW TO SECURE OUTHAUL FOR EASY ADJUSTMENT

Another common failing is to use light cotton or nylon line for the outhaul, and to tie a simple square knot loop (see illustration). Cotton and nylon stretch too much, and the loop with a square knot is hard to adjust precisely. For a better system, use dacron (1/8) and tie it as shown. Also use line as shown instead of the metal clip (for the tack fastening), since this enables you to adjust more quickly for more tension in heavy winds and less tension for light winds.

*Go for the Gold*

For the boom adjustment, you should have considerably less tension than on the gaff. For light weather this will probably mean a looseness that will cause the scallop effect—which looks awful but seems to work better. The boom adjustment will also do quite a bit for controlling the leach. You can see this by setting up your sail on land and trimming it as if you were sailing.

Most of the leaches on the Sunfish sails are pretty sad to look at. Not having battens, they tend either to hook in or flop off. As is true in other classes, a tight leach is better in light conditions, particularly when there is a slop. But you must be very careful not to overtrim with a tight leach, because this will shoot the wind off to windward and kill you. Of the two extremes a loose leach, even a flapping leach, is to be preferred, because you will gain more in a heavy wind with a loose leach than you will lose in a light wind. My sail at the 1970 world championship seemed to be flatter than most, and the leach was distressingly loose. I paid the penalty in the early light-wind races, where others definitely had better speed. But by carefully not overtrimming I was able to hang in there. And when it blew I had speed and control where boats with tighter leaches were fighting a big heeling moment. The ideal is to have a sail that with normal tension on the boom has a firm leach, with loose tension has a tight leach, and with hard tension has a loose leach. If you can't achieve that, err on the side of looseness.

### Position of Halyard on the Gaff

This subject is rather more complex than it appears. I can give you the measurement which I have arrived at as best, but it is important to understand here the reasons why, because adjustments on either side might be desirable depending on your weight.

My first theory was that since the Sunfish is underrigged, I should carry the sail as high as possible in order to get it up where there is more wind. The lower on the gaff you fasten the halyard, the higher the sail.

This theory seemed right, and the offwind performance was fine, but to windward the boat just seemed dead. The best explanation is that the lower you position the halyard, the more unsupported gaff is exposed. The more unsupported the gaff is, the more it bends. The more it bends, the flatter the sail. So in order to raise the sail you pay the penalty of a flatter sail—and it simply is not worth it.

What about the reverse? Well, the lower you carry the sail, the higher your halyard fastening must be. This supports the gaff more—which means less bending, and hence a fuller sail. I had this dramatically proved to me in one light-wind race, when my halyard knot slipped up on the gaff and the whole rig came down to deck level. Since the wind was light, it figured that I had had it— less wind at water level, blanketing effect of ocean swells, etc. Imagine my surprise when I started walking through the fleet, eventually passing the leader—a guy who usually beats me in light winds.

For a while I thought I had a real breakthrough. I reasoned that the much publicized end-plate effect of having the sail close to the deck must be doing something special. I had proved that it worked in light winds, and for heavy winds I would be lowering the center of effort more, making the boat easier to hold flat, which seemed to offer the best of both worlds.

Well, it didn't really. The good performance of this on deck rig in light winds is probably due to the previously mentioned fact that the high halyard position gives more support, thus permitting less bend, thus avoiding any flattening of the sail. This combination works directly against you in heavy winds, where the inability to flatten the sail hurts more than the lower center of effort can help. So a compromise position is better, and I'll get to that.

### Position of Gooseneck on Boom

When you start with an open mind, several possibilities present themselves here. If we move the gooseneck position aft we get more low sail area forward. This should help the helm and also should give the boom a negative angle, which is supposed to be helpful. Unfortunately, it doesn't seem to work out that way. The foretriangle area manages to be a rather inefficient piece of sail in any case, and therefore moving it forward doesn't do much good. If we move the gooseneck all the way forward on the boom, we in effect make the gaff almost vertical, and this approximates a Marconi rig, generally conceded to be the most efficient. It also drastically reduces the foretriangle area, which we have seen is rather ineffective. And by swinging the whole rig up, we put more sail area higher up, where there's more wind. Beautiful. Except that doesn't seem to work too well, either. And downwind in a breeze the boat really gets out of hand.

After much fooling around and seemingly endless theorizing, I arrived at the following measurements as best for me:

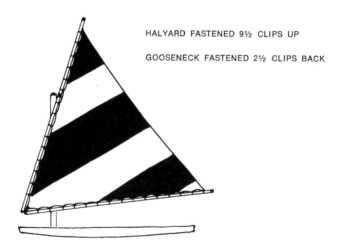

HALYARD FASTENED 9½ CLIPS UP

GOOSENECK FASTENED 2½ CLIPS BACK

Remember that these are the adjustments for a 165-pound sailor, who hikes hard and goes to 190 pounds with sweatshirts in a blow. If you weigh more, or hike less, these adjustments may not be right for you. But they won't be far off.

*Go for the Gold*

## Traveler Adjustment

As far as I know, I was the first to experiment successfully in important races with the idea of tying your mainsheet with a loose bowline to the traveler wire, rather than staying in the center wire loop. This is legal because you are not adding to or subtracting from the prescribed equipment. It works better for the same reasons that a sliding traveler works better on any boat—with the traveler out you trim down sooner, thus getting a flatter sail at a better angle for heavy winds. But the Sunfish rig is asymmetrical, so you must be careful how you put this into practice. To understand how it works, let's take a look at two Sunfish from above, one rigged with the boom on the port side, the other with the boom rigged on the starboard side of the mast. Most people put the boom to port, making starboard tack the slightly faster tack, particularly in lighter winds. I do this because I like the extra drive right around the start when you are normally on starboard tack.

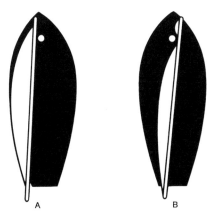

A                    B

*The Sunfish*

As you can see by the diagram, in situation A you have a considerably fuller sail, set considerably farther to leeward. If you use the center loop of the wire and trim to the same spot on both boats, you end up with a drastically different adjustment in terms of sail draft and sail angle. The best way to equalize trim for both tacks is to make the bowline loop in your mainsheet and tie it to the port side of the traveler (with the boom port side rig)—loose enough to slide but tight enough not to pass over the wire loop at the center of the traveler. This gives you a sliding traveler for starboard tack and a center rig traveler for port tack.

It didn't take people very long to catch on to the advantages of this little gimmick, but it is not quite the panacea that most want to believe. In lighter winds it is not good to have this outside traveler adjustment for starboard tack. So if the wind goes light and you are stuck with the sliding traveler, you have a problem. As a partial remedy you can gently pull the boom in by hand, and the mainsheet will stick on the traveler in roughly the position you want. But if the wind looks light from the start you might just as well tie the center loop.

These adjustments fairly well set up the rig, and with this arrangement if you just sail her reasonably well you should be able to stay with anybody, and to beat most.

Here are some other simple gear ideas that I use on the Sunfish:

• A mainsheet jam cleat is indispensable to effective windward work. Without this jam cleat you are constantly easing the sail out unconsciously.

• After you have tied the halyard to the gaff, with either a clove hitch or a rolling hitch, tape it to avoid slippage.

• Rig the halyard so as to get a more functional boom vang. This is very important for surfing, because when you give that quick trim for quick thrust you have to have a vang. Otherwise the trim is spongy—the boom just rides up and there is no transfer of power to a thrust forward.

• Make sure the leading edges of your dagger board and rudder are round and as absolutely smooth and even as you can make them within the rules. It is a good idea to use plastic or rubber pads inside the end of the trunk to keep the board from getting nicked fore and aft.

Sailing the Sunfish properly takes a bit of getting used to. The boat is very easy to stall and very hard to unstall. You will stall if you trim too close or heel too much. You will stall if you make excessive helm movements. You will stall if you pinch, or take the waves at the wrong angle. Above all, you must always keep this boat footing. If you go below a certain speed, the small area of the dagger board and rudder do not seem to hold the boat, and you drift to leeward in a most distracting manner.

## Heavy-Wind Tactics

As in any dinghy, you have to keep the Sunfish flat to windward. Most people heel too much, especially in the puffs, and you can see them fade sharply to leeward against the boat that is hiked flat. Once you get the Sunfish rolling you can point her rather than drive, but this must be carefully keyed to the wave pattern.

There is one particularly dangerous heel-drift sequence to avoid in the Sunfish. When you let the boat heel too much, the flat bottom is exposed, and when the wind hits this you heel even more and get blown to leeward faster than you would believe. Even worse, this same exposed flat bottom surface also gets hit by a big wave which knocks you off the leeward about 10 feet more in one swoop. So you must anticipate and parry the puffs. Give a maximum hike just before the puff hits, so you have maximum leverage and a little windward roll going for you. If she still starts to heel, shiver the sail with a helm luff to windward. If she still heels, let out the sail. Do anything to keep that flat bottom from getting up into the wind.

When a big wave bears down on you, the tendency is to bear off to get enough drive to push through. The trouble here is that when most people do this they also let the boat heel a bit, so the big wave gets a real whack at that exposed flat bottom —and the result is that the bow gets badly knocked off to leeward. Better to head up at the very last second and present the smallest possible profile to the wave. Of course you must have good way on to do this, and right after you punch through you must hike out and bear off again to regain speed. The slide down the back side of the wave can help you do this. If you practice, it will all become a rhythm that you don't have to think about.

At an early stage, I noticed that heavy winds caused most Sunfish skippers to come badly apart. Lots of the skippers who were excellent technicians in light or medium winds seemed to lose all their finesse in a blow. So I concentrated on developing heavy-wind control, because it was apparent this would pay big dividends, which it did.

In the world championships I was often able to start from dead behind a boat and work straight through to windward. The only sailor I was not able to grind down in this fashion was Joerg Bruder, the superb Finn sailor. We were just about equal in speed to windward, but my lighter weight gave me an edge off the wind that was probably decisive.

Develop your heavy-wind technique and you will learn to look forward to a blow. There are none of the fickle bad breaks of lighter winds, and hard work will almost certainly earn you a good place.

The Sunfish really likes a breeze, and the hull shape lends itself very nicely to extended surfing. Jibing in heavy winds is a piece of cake, since this boat gets very stable when it is planing. Go-abouts are not so simple, and the mainsheet should be uncleated so you can ease off and accelerate on the new tack.

# The Snipe

*T*he *Snipe* is, after the Sunfish, the largest racing
class, and in terms of true world-wide participa-
tion it is the most popular one-design boat. It
is also one of the most misunderstood boats, often
held in quite low esteem by yachtsmen who
consider it to be old-fashioned and low in performance. The IYRU shares the ignorance of this view,
and subsequently the Snipe has never been granted
the Olympic status which its unmatched international acceptance should long ago have earned.

The quickest cure for the critics and the cynics
would be to put them in a modern Snipe in a
competitive fleet. The cynics would find the Snipe a
very responsive boat, and the critics would
probably find themselves badly in the tank.

In recent years the story of superior performance

in the Snipe could be abbreviated to "The Brazilians and Earl Elms." The Brazilians, notably Erik and Axel Schmidt, dominated decisively for at least six years, and, having frequently followed them around the course, I can testify that theirs was no fluke performance. Conrad and Piccolo have also been outstanding for Brazil, particularly in the reaching department.

The present master of the class, however, is undeniably Earl Elms, five times U.S. champ and current world champion. The California Keg first built his own Snipe, which won the U.S. Nationals handily, and then, in conjunction with Herb Shear of Chubasco boats, brought out a fiberglas production model that continues to dominate the top ranks. Elms sails are the best Snipe sails on the market, again reflecting Earl's innovations. Finally, he has designed a new aluminum mast which has proved to be just that important little bit better than the standard Proctor. In short, nobody in the class comes close to combining the practical expertise Elms has in the Snipe hull, spar, and sails. This kind of composite knowledge is very tough to beat, particularly since he sails well to boot.

My advice to serious Snipe sailors is quite simple. Buy a Chubasco boat, rig it with a Cobra mast and Elms sails, and set it up to the measurements which Earl quite freely provides.

I realize that this is a pretty straight commercial, but I will be happy to make a similar endorsement as soon as somebody else shows similar prowess. After all, there is no sense in ignoring performance facts.

For international regattas the Snipe has now reduced its weight by 44 pounds to a total 381 pounds. This was a good move and long overdue, despite the shrieks and moans of the traditionalists who see any change as heresy.

What can I tell you about the Snipe other than the none-too-novel advice to copy Earl Elms? Distressingly little.

Actually I've got lots of ideas, and since I've always placed well in the Snipe, they could have a certain validity. But let's be true to the formula and go straight to the top for advice. We can publish our views as soon as we beat Elms.

# The Finn

*P*erhaps the most exacting class **of all is the Finn,**
because it demands physical strength, endurance,
and dexterity along with considerable tuning
perception—the latter much more than the sim-
plicity of the rig would indicate. The Finn is a very
rewarding boat from the point of view of experimentation, and offers great opportunities for
in-race as well as pre-race adjustments.

Above all, a certain toughness of mind and spirit
are essential in the Finn. Pain is an integral part
of the performance. In fact in heavy winds you
power the boat by pain, and your speed varies in
accordance with your willingness to suffer. It
follows that Finn sailors tend to be a class apart,
who love the boat for the very hardships that make
others wince and shake their heads. One of the

chief advantages of learning to sail the Finn competitively is that afterward every other class seems relatively easy. You feel almost sinfully comfortable in other boats. For this reason Finn sailors make excellent crews—they really understand the benefits of hiking and hard work.

More than in any other boat the physical characteristics of the skipper have to be looked on as part of the equipment in the Finn. For all-weather performance the 180–190 pound range seems best. It is true that a skillful 140-pounder may do very well in the light stuff, but he will be totally out of contention in over 15 knots of breeze. You can try to compensate with a more flexible mast, but this costs you ability to point—and the lack of weight will kill you in the end anyway.

While the long, lanky build can obviously stretch out farther for better hiking leverage, the short stocky build seems better able to take the strains of sustained hard hiking. The best Finn hiker that I have ever seen is Ron Jenyns of Australia, who is about 5 feet 7 inches and probably weighs about 185 pounds. Ron has heavy arms, chest, and shoulders, and powerful legs. Bruder of Brazil and Mankin of Russia also represent this type, and the relation of their similar builds to the similarity of their success is not at all coincidental. In a breeze, he who hikes best sails fastest in the Finn.

The 210-plus-pounders have a definite edge when it is really honking, but they also give away a lot in the marginal planing conditions off the wind.

A notable exception here is Peter Barrett. Pete is, in my opinion, the best heavy-wind Finn sailor around. He is also a threat in the medium stuff, but this is because he is a particularly smart sailor.

A slightly lighter but equally strong sailor like Joerg Bruder is able to hang in there to windward in a blow, and off the wind he really turns it on. Joerg manages to look more at home in the Finn than anyone I know, even in the hairiest conditions. In a 35 MPH stomper he moves around with an animal grace that is very disconcerting to those fully occupied with mere survival.

For those of you in the 150- to 160-pound range, I can only recount my personal experiences. At 160 pounds I felt that I was competitive with the best of them in winds up to 12 knots. Under those wind velocities I won races at the North American championships, and placed second in the third race of the Olympics at Acapulco. But my overall record in the class is somewhat indifferent because I always dropped badly when the wind blew over 15 knots. Which somehow it always does, especially when you are hoping it won't.

With superb conditioning it is possible for a 170-pounder to compete in a breeze by carrying from 50 to 100 pounds of sweatshirts. Carl van Dyne of the U.S. manages to do this remarkably well.

The Finn is a great boat, probably the toughest of all the popular class boats to sail well. It forces total development of all your sailing skills, and the penalty for miscalculation is swift and wet.

I believe it is no accident that Paul Elvström began his unmatched sailing career in the Finn. Every serious sailor could profit by some training time in this exacting single-hander where the competition is as tough as the boat itself.

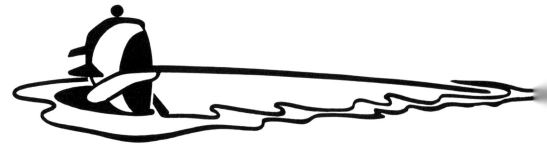

# Jibing a Finn

*ibing a Finn* calls for a special description because it is a special experience. Whereas in most boats a jibe is normally just another routine maneuver, in the Finn this move assumes heroic proportions, and provides lessons in humility that have made strong men weep.

If you've never jockeyed a Finn in a breeze over 25, this will mean nothing to you, but if you have, you are automatically a soul brother. Here's a typical sequence:

You round the windward mark with a nice 90-yard lead. The wind has been coming up steadily and is now gusting to 25. Vang down, board up, cunningham off, ass out, kazoom—you're off on a screamer. Sheets of spray and wild exhilaration as you blast out to a wider lead. And then suddenly, before you know it, there it is, the reaching mark. "By golly, hot damn, gee whiz, we better get set for the old jibe. The *jibe!*" Brow furrows, vision clouds, muscles stiffen, and a childlike whimper slips from your strong Nordic lips.

"Steady, boy, there's nothing to this. We'll just wait for a little lull." This naive hope is quickly extinguished by a glance aft, which reveals a solid mass of hissing whitecaps racing down to join you in your moment of truth.

"Well, we'll just get the board up a bit like Elvström says, so she'll slide to leeward and not trip." So you up the board six inches—a precaution your Finn greets with a wild, sickening lurch to windward. Only a desperate jab of the tiller and a frantic yank on the main keep you from instant oblivion via the famous Finn windward wipe-out, or "death roll."

Now the buoy is right off the port bow, and the puff hits full force. Down on your knees you plunge, neatly incising razor-like slashes on your legs from either the bailers or the hiking-strap mounting. Somehow straddling and backing into the tiller, you start the fateful arc. "My God, the vang—let off the vang!" (Failure to do this is a direct invitation to decapitation of the most primitive sort.) Shredding your knuckles to the bone you manage to cast off the vang. You haul in on the sheet—"Jibe ho!" But wait, she isn't jibing, and instead she slows down to a queasy stall and hangs there, midst a sudden and unnatural silence. "Get over there, you mother," and you haul

*Go for the Gold*

manfully on the sheet and rejam the tiller around.

And then she comes—that malevolent boom, screeched across the deck by a thousand devils. From long practice, you deftly duck your head and bear off slightly in perfect textbook style, counteracting the momentum of the turn. Except you forget about your elbow. . . . When you bore off, you quite naturally raised your elbow several inches for added leverage on the tiller—an innocent and seemingly minor oversight that would go unnoticed in most boats. No such luck in the Finn. With unerring accuracy the boom seeks the very point of your elbow and fetches it a smash that would make Tarzan gasp. In addition to the excruciating pain, this timely blow effectively numbs the entire arm, causing a critical delay in your downward correction.

It's all over but the jeering. The boom, which has already so cruelly punished you, now seeks to bury itself in the leeward bow wave. Your noble steed slops to a stop, sail pinned to the water. Sensing a kill, the wind shrieks its delight at a higher pitch. A la the illustration on page 64 of Elvström, you hurl yourself over the windward side to save your craft. But of course you aren't Elvström, so rather than sliding harmlessly to leeward, you dump ignominiously, quite probably fouling the mark in the process.

The rest is almost too painful to recount. Your competitors rocket by like dervishes, and since you know their control is marginal at best, moving around so as to right your boat is like stepping casually out on a California freeway. Beyond that, your centerboard has in all likelihood retreated up the trunk, leaving you the unhappy prospect of hanging by your fingernails from the slot, till your weary craft concedes and flops back up.

Someone should make a close-up movie of Finns at the jibing mark, if only to provide drama students with a study of how a man's expression can change in a flash from stark terror (before the jibe) to mad glee (if the jibe is successfully completed).

Actually the Finn jibe becomes a great equalizer, since it fells the high and mighty as readily as the tail-ender. And the saving grace is that after the Finn jibe all jibes in other classes become a piece of cake, to be executed with insolent insouciance.

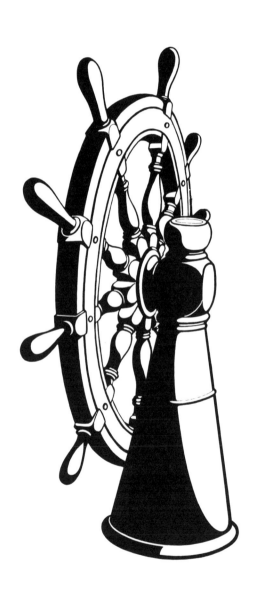

# The Role of the Skipper

*W*hat is the most effective role of the skipper in getting and using crew advice? As a businessman, my reaction is to listen carefully to other opinions, on the grounds that they might well be right and a better judgment can be made from an input that considers several viewpoints. This is dangerously sound logic. Like a lot of things in sailing, it doesn't quite work out as well as it sounds. Out on the water there is much to be said for the efficiency of total dictatorship.

I have generally been blessed with smart crews who are good sailors in their own right and whose opinions I respect. And I have frequently asked and used their advice as a supplement, or even a crutch, to my own judgment. Yet my performance as a single-handed sailor has always been slightly better than my performance in crew boats. I have thought about this, and my conclusion is that the regular asking of advice merely results in a compromise policy that multiplies the probability of error.

Look what happens. Everybody has some percentage of mistakes built into his overall performance—it's the guy who makes the fewest mistakes who wins. And each skipper has a performance profile—he generally makes $x$ number of good decisions and $y$ number of bad decisions. The ratio of $x$ to $y$ varies from race to race, but not as much as you might think. And this ratio to a large degree depends on a self-corrective device whereby the skipper's mind absorbs and compensates for errors.

Crew advice, however well meant and well founded, often upsets this delicate mechanism. You ask for advice at doubtful and critical moments: "Should we hold on this tack?" "Should we split to the other side?" Now, your own computer over the entire course will give you $x$ good moves and $y$ bad moves. If at critical moments you call in another computer, you're liable to catch him in his $y$ cycle of bad moves—which gives you the worst of both worlds.

If you are the skipper, your overall judgment performance should be better, however slightly, than your crew's. If it is not, then he should be skipper or chief tactician (this is not a bad plan, and there is nothing to say that the crew shouldn't call the shots and the helmsman merely steer). If you have a group of steady competitors to measure against, it is worth trying races where you call all the shots, where your crew calls all the shots, or where you combine decisions. Let the results decide.

I still feel there is an inherent danger of compromise in a policy of consulting. You unconsciously react to suggestions in a desire to accommodate a respected opinion, and this throws off your computer. I believe that democratically combined decisions do not necessarily mean added strength in a sailboat race. Out on the water, the best sailor should be an automatic majority of one.

For the benefit of the very powerful crew's union, I hasten to add that the best policy toward the crew is more than just "Shut up and hike." The crew should provide a constant flow of information as to what is happening in the race, plus observations on trim, speed, and wind shifts. You should counsel with your crew on a general game plan, and ask him to remind you when you deviate. CREW: "We said we were going to cover Charlie, and he just split to starboard." SKIPPER: "Yeah, but we're on a lift." CREW: "Let's not be greedy. The idea is to beat Charlie. Remember, we agreed . . ." SKIPPER: "Okay, okay, ready about. Get that damn jib in, get your ass out there. . . ."

# The Professionals

*I*t is an inescapable fact that sailboat racing in the popular one-design and Olympic class is increasingly dominated by the "professionals." By my own definition, "professional" means anyone who devotes full time to sailing or activities related to sailing. This includes sailmakers, boatmakers, mastmakers, naval architects, sailors supported by the government, and those wealthy enough to make sailing a full-time hobby.

Many people bemoan the fact that the professionals have deprived the sport of its amateur purity, and made it impossible for the average weekend sailor to compete with serious hopes of winning. Undeniably it must be accepted that the sailmaker who daily works at the business of making faster sails, and who can take business time and money for the research and competition that produces better sails, has an edge on the average hack who must spend his time selling insurance, cars, or whatever.

The counter-argument here is that most of these sailmakers were already excellent sailors when they went into business and that they are merely exercising their democratic right to do their own thing, probably at considerable economic sacrifice versus an "outside" job.

As I see it, it's a standoff. The pros have an unquestionable advantage, but not enough to make it fair or possible to exclude them. So the problem becomes how to cope with the reality of their advantage, and one of the best first steps in that direction is to stop crying about it.

Once you take this positive stance, you will find that most of the professionals can be extremely helpful to you. After all, they are in effect working for you all the time, since you can selectively buy the products which summarize their research and skill. Their business is to make you go faster. Moreover, they are for the most part extremely generous with their expertise. Guys like Earl Elms, Pete Barrett, Joerg Bruder, and Herbert Raudaschl will, I've found in my experience, freely share their knowledge with you, and in fact spend far more time on your individual problems than their nominal profit per unit sale could possibly justify.

The professional will probably always have a deeper technical knowledge than you can acquire. If you just shrug your shoulders in resigned despair, he will beat you with this deeper knowledge. But if you will take the trouble to study what he has learned, and buy selectively from the whole range of products of the best professionals, you will end up out on the course with a composite of equipment that is as good as, or better than, any pro's.

And given equality in equipment, you can, by reading and thinking, develop your sailing technique to the point where you are fully competitive.

As a veteran of the world's oldest profession was overheard complaining in a bar, "It's really tough to compete with all these dedicated amateurs."

# The Best Sailors

*Small boat* sailors are better than big boat sailors. Well, they are. If this sounds unduly provocative it is only to balance the record, which has long pretended—via disproportionate publicity—that the winners of the America's Cup and the Bermuda Race are the world's best sailors. While it is certainly possible that they could be, it is also quite likely that they are not.

To prove this is so is as simple as looking at the record, which shows any number of small boat sailors moving into the winning ranks in bigger boats, but a distinct scarcity of big boat skippers competing downward with any success. The clincher comes when they both meet on common ground—even common ground clearly favoring the big boats—such as the Congressional Cup.

This is a series sailed around the buoys in closely matched big class boats, such as Cal 40s and Columbia 50s. The boats are drawn for and are as evenly matched as possible. The big boat boys are there, but the winners, as far back as I can remember, are the dinghy sailors and their dinghy crews. In 1968 it was Finn sailor Henry Sprague, and in 1969 Snipe sailor Argyll Campbell.

The reason for this, and the point in bringing up the whole subject, has to do with the conditioning value of wide-open competition. Big boat sailors, like polo players, suffer from an artificially limited climate of competition. They are insulated by great wads of dough from abrasive brushes with the unwashed public.

Which makes for a very genteel atmosphere at the club, but doesn't really prove much beyond establishing which rich kid has the fastest equipment.

If you really want to find out where you are as a helmsman and tactician, jump into the smallest standard class with the biggest number of competitors. If you win, you'll know it was you and not your checkbook. And the tougher skills you acquire in this tougher, more open competition will stand you in excellent stead no matter what you sail thereafter. The bigger the boat, the more emphasis there is on the equipment. The smaller the boat, the more emphasis there is on the man.

So big boat skippers who want to sharpen up their touch would do well to drop back periodically into dinghies. Bad habits show up quicker in small boats (it's really hard to capsize a 12-Meter), and for that reason the indispensable sense of feel is more quickly and more acutely developed in smaller craft.

All this reads like a big put-down on the big boat skippers, and that really isn't the idea. Big boat racing is in many ways a different bag, where organizational ability, knowledge of navigation and equipment, and weather-forecasting ability are as important as the actual helmsmanship.

Granted. But I still say, the smaller the boat and the bigger the class, the better the sailor.

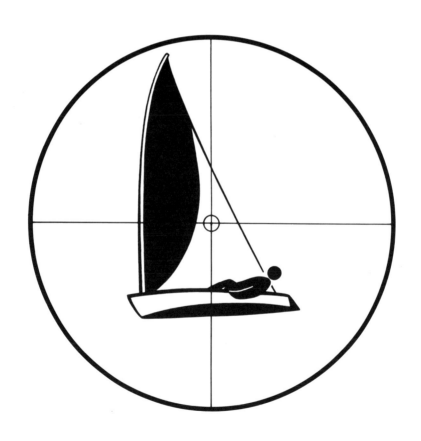

# Influence by Effluence

"Covering" is a phrase that is loosely thrown about to describe the tactics of preserving a lead or restraining a threatening competitor. I think the word "covering" has an overly defensive ring, which not coincidentally is the mistaken way most sailors go about using this ploy.

The best description I know was heard in a complaint from a sailor who found himself frustrated in the latter stages of a race by a very adequate cover job. "Every time I turned around, the bastard was squatting on my face," quoth the victim.

While apologizing for possible indelicacy of phrasing, I have to applaud this visceral prose as depicting far more graphically what really goes on —or should go on—in this most offensive of countermoves.

Perhaps we should first of all separate "loose cover" (we'll use that word for propriety) and "close cover," which are two quite different things. "Loose cover" essentially means stationing yourself so that you can be sure you will get basically the same wind as a boat, or group of boats, behind you. In loose cover you do not seek to interfere with following boats; rather, you merely want to ride herd on them.

"Close cover" is called for when a feared or respected competitor challenges from close behind. The first thing to get straight about close cover is that, to make it work right, you have to turn on an active desire for malicious mischief. Forget about Corinthianism and start working up a cold professional hate. After all, *that sonofabitch is trying to pass you,* which is an enormous personal insult and must be treated as such.

In righteous indignation you are going to crap upon him, in the sincere hope that from this he will acquire new and proper respect and refrain from further impertinences.

Your weapons are wind interference and wave disturbance. They must be applied with Chinese patience, Italian guile, and Nazi efficiency. Since this guy is now gaining to the point that you can feel his hot breath, you cannot be content with merely riding herd on the same tack. You have to push him back, hopefully annoying and discouraging him in the process, since both these emotions will impair his subsequent ability to attack effectively. The closer he gets, the better the weapons at your disposal will work—in fact, they only work within an arc of four or five mast lengths. The problem here is that since you must get this challenger into your circle of influence in order to damage him, the very proximity that will make him vulnerable also puts him dangerously close to a breakthrough, where he starts to work on you.

The "tacking duels" which you see and read about are often taken to be examples of covering, when actually they are examples of frustrated covering.

When you cross tacks and then tack on somebody's wind, and he immediately tacks, you have not hurt him. You are merely signing up for a contest to see who can lose the least by frequent go-abouts. There is nothing wrong with this, since frequently it's your only option, and if your maneuvers are smooth, and his are bad, you can gain precious yardage. When employing this tactic it is most important to know, via the compass, which is the favored tack. Since by being ahead you control the timing and can force him to tack, you must try always to push him onto the lousy tack.

If you see an opponent coming up, and you have to tack to get on him, it is often better to cross and not tack directly on his wind—since he will usually tack right away and you can't tack again immediately. Instead, carry on until you're not on his wind but just up to windward—and then go about. Chances are he'll hold, because you're not affecting his wind. As soon as you get squared away, ease off the wind a notch and start to drive

*Influence by Effluence*

off onto his wind. You will lose some ground by this, but the reward is that you really stay in control of the situation.

He can see you coming, but there is not much he can do. When you finally cross his wind, you will blanket him totally from close range, and unless he tacks immediately he will lose drastically. If he tacks, you must tack too, right away, so that you blanket him again just as he tries to pull away on the new tack. It is at this point that you should be able to punish him harshly. Don't let him off the hook. If he bears off, you bear off, if he tacks, you tack. Make sure you keep squatting on his face.

Some technicians might observe that there is a rule about bearing off on an opponent. In my opinion this rule is virtually unenforceable. Given the different slants of wind in different areas, and the different windward styles of each helmsman (some pinch—others drive), it's an impossible offense to prove.

It is a very tough windward situation when an opponent starts to work up on you from behind. He is heartened as much by his gains as you are disheartened—it seems inevitable he will burst through. At this point you must not get psyched. You have stayed ahead of him thus far, so you must be just as fast. Think that he's just getting close enough so you can hit him. Then hook into him and stay with him.

Remember, it is far better to be in control of a guy who is close behind than to have a 300-yard lead on somebody who is out of your control.

*Go for the Gold*

If you keep your cool you can hold the former, but the latter can luck into better wind at any moment, leaving you no recourse.

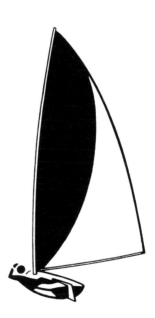

# Thoughts from Deep in the Tank

*T*o *achieve* the proper mood for this chapter, I waited for a regatta where I was really badly tanked. Wiped out, stomped into the ground, vanquished. Because I think there is a special perspective to be gained from tasting, firsthand, the kind of black despair that a bad series of races produces. The symptoms are painfully familiar to us all.

You've got a serious case of the slows. You just aren't moving, and you don't know why. Your confidence wavers and flutters wildly. You wonder if you really know anything, after all these years of sailing. Everything you try turns to crap. Guys you know you can beat walk all over you, and revel in so doing. You try to be a gracious loser, but you're so browned off you even fail at that.

The solution, and it's not an easy one, is to go back to the basics. Vince Lombardi used to say that football was, despite its many subtleties, a very simple game. Block and tackle well—you win. Do it poorly—you lose. So when the Packers blew a game, Lombardi didn't fret about this bad play or that awful fumble. Rather, he went back to stressing the simple execution of crisp blocking and tackling, on the very sound theory that if you do those things right, everything else will tend to fall into place.

So it is with sailboat racing. If you think back through your latest disaster you usually find that, beyond specific mishaps, general sloppiness merely exacted its general toll. The cure is to go back out on the water and grind away at the basics.

I recall once doing very poorly in a Finn regatta, and since my favorite mast had been broken in shipment, I was totally down and felt I just didn't have it. After the race, I was limping home with my tail between my legs when I noticed one of the top finishers setting out for some extra practice. I forced myself to go out and do battle again. And sure enough, in the informal but grimly fought sparring that ensued, I was just as fast. *But the reason I was just as fast was that I was sailing and hiking harder than I had during the actual race.* And this, of course, is the real answer. A bad shift or an early dumb move can put anybody into the tank. But the actual distance you are behind is not as costly as the lapses in concentration that these early reverses cause.

The real test of the championship skipper is the ability to rally back from early disaster. This means bearing down when every bone tells you to give up.

Don't just sit there. Blast your way out of the tank.

# Situations

*T*he *chief benefit* of experience is not the acqui-
sition of great stores of hoary wisdom, but the
gradual buildup of a handy catalog of situations.
With experience you don't have to reason out a
solution for x set of circumstances; rather, you
refer by reflex to your catalog, and fish out the
parallel situation that tells you what to do.

You start your catalog with an ABC series of
basic yachting disasters—bad landings, capsizes,
collisions, etc. Nautical no-no's are generally memorable because they are closely attached to, and
followed by, sharp sensory reprisals. . . . Just as in
boxing, where the need for never lowering your
righthand guard is neatly established not so much
by the pronouncement of that rule as by the pain
of the resounding left hook that follows its neglect.

By this same token I can still recall my first accidental jibe . . . in a Barnegat Bay Sneakbox. This is a murderously unbalanced little craft, and an accidental jibe in it can be an awesome experience, especially when you are ten years old. The boom rises up, kisses the gaff, and then, cocked from this backswing, roars across the deck in a roundhouse sweep, carrying away all the boat's rigging and most of the skipper's confidence.

Events like this rapidly develop an awareness of consequences—and being able quickly to project foreseeable events into probable consequences is what makes a good racing skipper.

So don't shrink from your memory of disastrous situations—rather, remember them in full detail. Pretty soon you'll have the most complete set of panic buttons in the fleet, neatly ordered so you can punch them quickly for a fast mental print-out.

# Goal to Go

*A*nybody can be beaten. That claim comes on
like half-time oratory, but gaining such conviction
is surprisingly vital to any hope of success in
sailing. Somehow if you sort of expect to be beaten,
you nearly always are.

How often have we all seen either newcomers
or chronic habitués of the bottom half right in
there on the first windward leg—their very proximity demonstrating their ability to keep pace? Yet
they seem to feel—and I've even heard them say,
in embarrassed self-consciousness—"What am I
doing up here?" And since the body will not long
support as fact what the mind believes to be fiction,
they blow.

Oddly enough, these sailors often seem more
concerned with fulfilling their own conviction of

failure than avoiding the failure itself. Having found themselves (inexplicably, in their own view) in the rarefied atmosphere of first place, they more than anything expect to be passed. They almost seem to want to be passed, and appear relieved to sink back to the more comfortable ranks of the rear.

Rid yourself of any such hangups, because they really get in the way.

If there is one characteristic which all winners share, it is impatience with, and intolerance for, losing. If you don't have this, you must develop it. Forget about learning to be a good loser—it's easier to learn to be a good winner.

Nobody is so good that on a given day he can't be beaten, and this applies to any sailor and any class I've ever heard of. The awe and the deference with which most winners are treated is one of the advantages they most rely on to win. Everybody gets out of their way, by subconsciously accepting the fact that they are coming through anyway.

Thus the top guys always seem to come up, even from the deep tank, propelled as much by the rest of the fleet's fixation with failure as by their own rejection of that failure.

Get tough, think big, and stop rolling over for number one. He puts his sails on the same way you do, and he can be had.

# The Ways of Wind
and Sea

$\mathcal{H}$*ere,* regrettably, we must put aside poetic allusions and romantic illusions. The wind is a wanton and the sea is a whore. Sometimes vice versa. Since they work in concert we are in effect dealing with a wanton whore.

This observation does not imply censure or cynicism, but merely a developed sense of reality. If the double damnation seems redundant, remember that a wanton whore is quite distinct from a reliable whore. The latter, though available to any man, could presumably be bought for special occasions for you alone. But your true wanton, which wind and sea combine to represent, will charge stupefying sums in equipment, and tempt you along with the insinuation that this exorbitant outlay will somehow guarantee a full savoring of her favors. Then she goes off with the garbage man in his garbage scow. And takes him round the world, or at least round the course, before your very eyes.

Yet if you slyly shift to cop this ploy, and try to make the grade on just your manly charm, she quickly becomes more whore than wanton, and passes you by for fat old men who have simply put their money on the line.

The important thing to keep in mind is that this wind-sea Carmen is infinitely wise in the ways of men, and though she must be wooed, she can never be won. You may desire her passionately, pay her excessively, and possess her occasionally, but you will never fully know her.

This lure of impossible conquest, plus the extravagant blue-green of her eyes, is the only logical explanation why, in a space age, otherwise sensible men will go to such lengths to carve and careen their way around small triangles of uncomfortable wet—at four knots.

If you do not share this idolatrous lust for wind and sea, you are lacking a key ingredient for yachting success. Because nothing short of nearsighted, and occasionally blind, worship will inure you sufficiently to the accumulation of insults to ego and pocketbook which your quest for gold must inevitably exact.

# Whither and Why the Quest

*H*aving exhorted you to *Go for the Gold—* and in the name of that Holy Grail lightened your ballast by several dollars—compassion calls for at least two bits of philosophy to restore a semblance of trim.

The reasons why men go down to the sea in ships have long baffled farmers, infidels, and weekend widows. Better authors than I have had a crack at this mystery, and if you have not read Conrad, Melville, or Masefield, you would do well to consider them as useful counterpoints which will help you fully savor a blunt Elvström truism.

From my own view, I happen to believe we take to the water in racing chips because this brings us back to the land in a way no shorebound course can. Sailing offers the sinfully attractive indulgence of combining recreation with restoration. It's a tonic that tastes good—a cure in a swinging sanatorium that's blessedly free of the landlocked logic from whence our troubles spring. Short of oral attentions from Raquel Welch, it's hard to think of a more intensely diverting therapy.

The racing competition? Well, that's the stone that sharpens our skills. And it takes sharpened skills to read the complex score of sights and sounds that weave wind and wave together. This is where the Sunday sailors and powerboat guys miss out. The same ocean is there for them, and, in fact, it's there in far greater comfort and convenience. But they're seeing it in black and white because they haven't been forced to develop the sensitivities that are needed to see all the colors of the sea spectrum. The saving grace is that they don't know what they are missing, and you can't really tell them because it's a different sort of language.

Like when, after a long hard drive from back in the pack, you finally close the lead boat on the last leg. He flops to cover, but that agile ape he has for crew finally butterfingers one, and you punch a bow free to leeward. Eating a little backwind gives skipper and ape further cause for pause, and then, just a hair short of the lay line, you lay on a classic go-about—one of those gems where she shoots into the wind like a javelin and clicks into the other slot without missing a beat. They cast a beseeching glance at the line, but they're short. But if they bear off and pass astern . . . ha, no way! Touché, checkmate, voilá!

Not too loud, because you know they know, you underscore their dilemma with a quiet call of "starboard." Anything more would be gauche—"starboard" says it all.

In this rare moment God's in his heaven, you're lifting to the mark, and all's right with the world. It's a moment laden with subtleties that are reserved for the racing sailor.

It matters little if this victory is as rare as the event itself is minor, or that it comes shadowed by a regular diet of lesser luck. Frequent despair is just part of your qualifying fee for the quest. And the quest, the getting there, is more than half the fun —it's *all* the fun, because the voyage, with its mixed bag of travails and triumphs, is the real gold.

*Whither and Why the Quest*

# Index

Reaching, 30–32, 55–58, 61–63; importance of, 55–56, 58; speed during, 55–58; tactics of, 61–63

Rig: adjustment of, 48; Marconi, 86. *See also* Sail.

Rowboat, 48

Royal Bermuda Yacht Club, 16

Rudder: smoothing of, on Sunfish, 89; during stalling, on Sunfish, 89; use of, 48

Sailor. *See* Crew; Skipper.

Sail: angle of, 46, 88; draft of, 75, 88; selection of, 23–24; of the Snipe, 94; of the Sunfish, 80, 88; trimming of, 57, 69, 87

Scandinavians, 48

Schmidt, Axel, 94

Schmidt, Erik, 94

Sea, unpredictability of, 139–140

Shear, Herb, 94

Sheet: angle of, 48; location of, 24. *See also* Mainsheet.

Skills, basic: emphasized in various classes, 74–76 (*see also* Finn; Snipe; Sunfish); importance of, 26

Skipper: decisions of, 110–111; motivation of, 139–140, 143–145; movement of, 57; movement of, during surfing, 69; performance of, 25–26; physical characteristics of, in the Finn, 98–99; professional, 113–115; professional, advice of, 48; role of, 57–58, 109–111; Scandinavian, 48; small boat, compared with big boat, 117–119; weight of, adjustments for, 83, 86

Snipe, 75, 93–95

Speed, 21–27; adjustment of sail for, *see* Sail; affected by start, 38; of the Finn, 97; how to judge, 46; loss of, while pointing, 47; on reaches, 55–58; in surfing, 66; of wind, 57; in windward sailing, 56

Sprague, Henry, 118

SS (skipper stupidity) factor, 16–17, 18

Stalling: in a Finn, 104–105; in a Sunfish, 89

Standardization of the Sunfish, 78–79

Star, 73–74

Starting, 35–43; importance of, 31–32, 35–40; premature, 41, 43; tactics of, 38–43

Stay: pinging of, 27; tension of, 24

Steering, during surfing, 65, 70

Strategy, 109–111; and boat speed, 22; role of crew in determining, 111; tacking, 123–124. *See also* Course, choice of; Covering; Passing; Starting.
Sunfish, 39, 75, 79–92
Surfing, 65–72; body, 66–67; on reaches, 56; in the Sunfish, 75, 89, 91; on a surfboard, 67–68

Tack fastening, 82
Tacking: clearance, 36; duels of, 123–124; equalizing trim for, in Sunfish, 88; purpose of, 52; starboard, in Sunfish, 87
Tempest, 40, 75
Tempo, race, 30
Threading the waves, 47–48
Thrust, 57
Traveler, 48; adjustment of, in Sunfish, 87–88; sliding, 87
Trimming, 57, 69, 87; effect of tuning on, 24
Tuning, 22-27; of the Finn, 97; of the Sunfish, 79–92

Van Dyne, Carl, 99
Vang, 104
Victory: attitude for, 12, 135–136; joys of, 144–145

Waves: bow, 46; breaks in, 67–68; choppy, 47, 72; formation of, 70; and heeling, 90–91; maximizing effect of, 56–57 (*see also* Surfing); pattern of, 47–48; threading of, 47–48; use of, in covering, 122
Weather, ability to forecast, 119
Weathering, 45, 46
Weight, skipper's: shifting of, 57, 69; adjustment for, 83, 86, 98–99
Wind: heavy, and Sunfish, 90–91; interference of, in covering, 122; shifts in, 31, 51–52; speed of, adjustments for, 46, 57 (*see also* Sails); speed of, and the Finn, 98–99; tacking on opponent's, 123–124; unpredictability of, 139–140; use of, in surfing, 65–66
Windward sailing, 30–31, 45–52; glamour of, 31, 45; in the Snipe, 75; styles of, 124. *See also* Covering.
Winning. *See* Victory.

*A Note on the Author*

Garry Hoyt lives in Santurce, Puerto Rico, where he is a senior vice-president with Young & Rubicam advertising agency. Born in Elizabeth, New Jersey, he studied at Colgate University and the American Institute for Foreign Trade, and served at sea with the Coast Guard. Mr. Hoyt now sails various classes of boats throughout the Caribbean, where he has been champion in the Finn, Snipe, and Sunfish Classes. He was World Sunfish Champion in 1970 and has placed third in the North American Finn and the World Snipe championships.